Highways, Ditches, and Dirt Roads

A Journey of Hope

ALFRED UNGER

WestBow Press books may be ordered through booksellers or by contacting:

WestBow Press
A Division of Thomas Nelson & Zondervan
1663 Liberty Drive
Bloomington, IN 47403
www.westbowpress.com
844-714-3454

Interior Image Credit: Alfred Unger, Diane Unger, John J. Unger

ISBN: 978-1-6642-5070-3 (sc)
ISBN: 978-1-6642-5071-0 (e)

Library of Congress Control Number: 2021923745

Print information available on the last page.

WestBow Press rev. date: 01/28/2022

WESTBOW
PRESS®
A DIVISION OF THOMAS NELSON
& ZONDERVAN

Highways, Ditches, and Dirt Roads

FOREWORD

There are many ways and reasons to write a foreword like this one for a dear friend. But none of them have worked for me.

And so, I will write to you, perched on the verge of reading Highways, Ditches and Dirt Roads.

Only today, Thanksgiving weekend, have I read the finished version of the book in your hand and understood why it took so long to make the trip.

Alfred's pain has been parallel to my own. And mine eclipsed his; until today.

In one sitting, the book is like passing a field on the highway, the symmetry and design of Alfred's story caught in an unexpected glimpse of hope and beauty. His fields were not planted by random distribution but rather, with observable intention and order, row upon row, line upon line.

And, by extension, my own.

Maybe you too will share in an experience of hope being restored. Who knows?

In a few moments, my friend will be inviting you to travel with him on a journey. His and yours.

Reluctantly, I have taken his advice to not hurry which was difficult but worthwhile.

With life-giving rhythm, Alf Unger has surfaced in so many lives like a drink of cold water on a hot day. For many of us, he has been an angel, albeit a very dusty one on occasion.

To say much more would be to give the story away too soon.

You will discover a blessing at the very end which was given to our family upon the death of our still-born son Paul Stanley. Alf and I met shortly after his tour of the same dark tunnel.

Within the hour, I will tell Alfred what I just told you and that, for the first time.

And now, it's your turn to go for a ride with Alfred Unger.

Take your time. Imagine the scenery which you may have seen yourself in the past.

But better still, accept his invitation to go behind his buttons into the heart.

And yours. Because that's the destination of his invitation to you.

Stan Biggs
Thanksgiving
2021

AN INVITATION

Come, my friend.

Come travel with me.

From the sand dunes of Southern California to the mountains of Alaska, and a thousand skies between, may these images and reflections open new horizons of hope for you as they have for me.

Resist the urge to move too quickly.

Rather, let your spirit rest at each scene, for the secrets within are not unraveled hastily.

The Lord Himself goes before you and will be with you; He will never leave you nor forsake you. Do not be afraid, do not be discouraged.

Deuteronomy 31:8 NIV

Winterhaven, California

DEDICATION

This work is dedicated to my many friends who have journeyed together with me. Sometimes it was for only a short period of time, and others are still beside me in some capacity. Some of you worked with your hands, some with a pen. Some were preachers. Some were teachers. Some were co-workers. Some were addicts. Some were singers. Some were dancers. Some were servers. Some were bosses. With some I broke my vows. With others, I celebrated family. Some were random strangers, if there is such a thing. Those of you who have crossed my path have left your mark.

Yet God has blessed this broken road.

To my three sons, Shaun, Carey, and Matthew: I am so proud of each one of you, for the men you have grown to be. No father could ask for more. Words cannot express the profound joy you give me. Thank you for who you are.

To my wife, Diane: You have stood with me always. For better and for worse, you have believed in me. You have cared for me. I love you for loving me. I would be lost without you. Thank you darling.

I owe my life to every one of you because without you, I wouldn't have made it this far. We've laughed together and we've cried together. We drank coffee and wine together. Other times it was whiskey, or rum. Sometimes we drank tequila. We loved and we fought. We won and we lost. We climbed and we stumbled. Thank you for journeying with me.

You are dearly loved; by me, but even more so, by a Heavenly Father who cherishes each one of you.

INTRODUCTION

The prayer of a righteous person is powerful and effective. (James 5:16 NIV) These words were penned by the brother of Jesus.

I'm not a righteous man, but God has chosen to answer some of my prayers anyway, and the fact that you are reading this right now is proof of that.

I was encouraged to write this by a number of friends who heard me speak. I am indebted to them for giving me a nudge toward this.

What follows is a collection of stories and thoughts from my life, gathered through many years, and frequently created while I was staring out from behind a windshield driving up and down the highway. These thoughts have also grown from times where I hit the ditch and journeyed along many dirt roads, both literally and figuratively.

These are conversations of hope amid the storms of life. They are meandering tales, trails, and views from my journey. My writing has often helped me as I have worked through challenges I faced. I hope you will find them helpful.

I offer this to you in hopes that it encourages you and challenges you to be your best, to grow, and to view the world with a larger heart as part of our global community.

CHAPTER 1   THE LILAC BUSH

I was eight when I first drove my father's truck.

We were living on a farm in Southern Alberta, and our crop of fresh peas had just been harvested. Our family consisted of Mom and Dad and their seven children; five brothers, and two sisters. I was third youngest.

Some of the family were at home shelling peas and getting them ready to freeze for winter and I was out in the field spreading the piles of vines the harvesters had left behind. There was a tractor and my Dad's truck out in the field.

Both needed to be brought home to the yard.

My older brother Melvin, had walked out to bring the tractor home. Once he got out to the field he also helped me get going with the truck with the instructions to turn off the ignition once I got to the yard.

I set off.

I carefully steered the 1952 Ford 1/2 ton across the field toward the dirt road that led home. This was about 1/2 mile from the yard. As I got to the road, I was beginning to feel more confident, and although I couldn't reach the pedals I was doing fine.

I was excited as I drove onto the yard. My chest must have been popping the buttons from my shirt. I had driven Dad's truck in from the field! I pulled up in front of the house while the rest of my family watched. I was looking at them, proudly beaming from ear to ear.

I can still see the expression on my father's face as he watched me drive directly into the lilac bush!

Rarely does life turn out the way we expect it to.

Years later I was married to my young bride, and we had two sons. Life was good.

Little did we suspect the tragedy that lay around the corner.

Sechelt, British Columbia

CHAPTER 2 THE TWINS

Fast forward a lifetime, and I find myself once again driving a truck, an 18 wheeler, and although this one is much bigger, I can reach the pedals. So far, I have avoided any more lilac bushes!

As I stare out the window, I hear the hum of the tires rolling the miles away and my mind drifts back over the years that brought me to this place.

Diane, and I were married exactly one week after I turned 21. She is exactly one year younger than I am. We share the same birthday. I was farming and with the summer farm schedules there were two possible dates for our wedding. One was our birthday, the other was a week later. At least this makes it easy to remember our anniversary!

Things were very good. We were involved in our local church and had a strong (young) faith in God. We sang in the choir on Sunday mornings and at one point I was asked to be the chairman of the church board. (I was wise enough to know that I wasn't wise enough to hold that position and turned it down.)

Our boys were growing. We made the decision to sell our interest in the farm and moved to our small town where we paid for our first home with cash. Several years later, we would sell it and invest in a business franchise that was a dismal failure, but for now it looked like our lives were blessed and completely together.

We wanted another child, and soon we were expecting. You can only imagine the excitement we felt when we learned we were expecting twins!

But then some concerns began to develop with Diane's pregnancy. Something was wrong. So we turned to our faith and prayed. We prayed as fervently as we knew how, yet the day came when we were told that there was no heartbeat that could be heard.

Yet we believed in a miracle. God would somehow protect our little ones. We prayed harder than ever.

A youth ministry that I was leading hosted an Amy Grant "Age to Age" concert with Michael W. Smith. When Amy sang her hit single "Friends", I was sure she was singing it just for me - for us. I was deeply encouraged. This would work out.

Two weeks later, our perfectly formed twin boys were delivered - stillborn.

We were devastated.

We didn't know where to turn. How could this have happened? We believed for our miracle. Our faith was strong.

And now our dream, and these precious little children, lay wrapped in white sheets on the hospital bed.

The next days, weeks, and months were a blur. Questions plagued our minds.

Where was God? Why had our babies died? Was our faith not strong enough? Had we not prayed enough? Had we not believed enough? What did we do wrong?

Neither of us pretended to be perfect. We knew that if this was some sort of judgement from God, we deserved it and far worse. Yet we had tried so hard to live in a way that would please Him.

This was the beginning of a long journey for me.

A year later, I cried for the first time since we had lost our twins, Michael and Gabriel.

My faith had been utterly shaken.

Penticton, British Columbia

Be still and know that I am God.

Psalm 46:10 NIV

CHAPTER 3 GOD AND ZEUS

I remember attending an adult Sunday School class where we were discussing the blessing of God on His righteous followers. "If you are righteous, God will bless you."

This tore at my heart. I knew I wasn't perfect but if perfection was the standard for God's blessing, how could anyone expect to receive it?

And what about Job?

It's an ancient story of a man that clearly honored God in his life. Scripture records even tell us that God brags about His servant, Job, and how blameless he is. Yet he was afflicted with all sorts of torment and lost everything! His friends suggest there is some deep sin in his life, but in the end, God vindicates him.

I mention this in the class.

What happened next is almost impossible to believe. It was as if the conversation was moving along, and when I spoke, the soundtrack just dropped out completely. As soon as I had finished, the conversation carried on as before. Nobody had heard anything I said. Not one comment; not one acknowledgment; not one response.

Unbelievable!

When we left church that day, I told Diane that I was not going back.

Who is this angry, judgmental God? And what hope have we of pleasing Him?

It was years before I began to see that my image of God was really the image of Zeus - an angry old man, who was looking for any chance to cast his spear of punishment on his enemies.

"God will get you for that!" God was always watching with angry displeasure on everything I did. He was our "Elf on the Shelf", "Gonna find out who's naughty, or nice." If you don't behave, you'll only get a lump of coal for Christmas.

Thunderous lightning from His flaming spear! This was a God to be feared!

This was Zeus.

So who is this God of Love that we hear about?

Elko, Nevada

CHAPTER 4 STARTING A DANCE ON THE WRONG FOOT

I have a confession to make.

It was during my time as church choir conductor that Diane and I decided to take dance lessons.

This might not seem to be a big deal, but we had both grown up in very conservative churches where dance was taboo. (Don't try to figure it out. It's just the way it was.) After much consideration, we had come to the conclusion that there was nothing wrong with dancing and we wanted to learn.

But dance classes were on Thursday night - the night of choir rehearsal.

That fall, the church was without a choir. They only knew that we had a "personal development class" that conflicted with choir practice, so we weren't available on Thursdays!

I still love dancing!

I've learned one thing about dancing. You've got to start on the right foot or everything goes wrong!

It's no different in our understanding of God.

I've realized that our understanding of the character of God is the most important thing, and we must get it right. Otherwise, our entire life is a dance that started on the wrong foot.

Oxnard, California

CHAPTER 5   OUR VIEW OF GOD

What is God REALLY like?

I've had hours to think about this. The isolation of the road has become my own private hermitage.

This question has been the biggest struggle in my life.

Here's what I know. Like a dance, if we get this answer wrong, everything else will also be wrong. Our entire worldview, our way of being in the world, our way of understanding life, and even our actions and reactions to events in our life, are all coloured by the answer to this question.

What is God REALLY like?

If we met face to face, what would our reaction be? Is God a "He"? Is God a "She"? Is gender even a consideration or is God a blend of the very best of each gender; "He" and "She" inside one "body"? This makes the most sense to me. God isn't "He" and also isn't "She" but is both "He" and "She" at the same time, in the same "Person".

Which then means God is a "Person". I also believe God is personal. This belief comes from my Judeo-Christian position. It is my worldview.

But this doesn't answer the question as to the character of a God of Love. If God is Love, it changes everything.

Lots of miles have rolled by on this one, so bear with me.

This statement does not say that God is loving. It says the very essence of God, is love.

Like a perfume that is spilled out, the fragrance, the essence, fills the room. It permeates everywhere and everything. If God is completely Love, then whenever we see love, we are actually seeing God's essence. God is in all love. All love holds the fragrance or essence of God, wherever we encounter it. Even when we distort it completely, the essence remains.

Therefore, if we live in love, we live in God, and when we live outside of love, we live outside of God.

On the one hand, love is irresistible. We are drawn to it like a moth to the flame. But on the other hand, we can resist love and turn away from it, but doing so leads us into a life of darkness and torment.

This we see repeatedly as we look around us. It may even be that this is the reason we say, "They have fallen in love".

The resulting darkness and torment is also evident when two people fall out of love. A broken heart is a physical pain.

The essence of Love (God) is all around us. It is clearly evident in the lives of people who live in love. The opposite is also evident. We choose moment by moment, which position we will live in.

But this still doesn't answer the question of how God (Love) interacts with us (me) on a daily basis in terms of how things go in my life. Yet maybe it does on a deeper level. That even when things do not go well, I am carried in Love and I can respond in love.

I'll think on this some more, and maybe I'll have other insights to share later. For now, this is all I've got.

Sutton, Alaska

CHAPTER 6   YOU BREAK IT, YOU BOUGHT IT

I've been thinking about this a lot more and it seems to me that love must be more than just a gushy feeling where misdeeds are simply overlooked or ignored.

Love must also include justice. Evil must be judged. Heaven isn't mandatory. We always have choice, but it's not about being "good enough."

I love the story I heard recently about a father who took his young son into a store to help him purchase a birthday gift for his mom. It was one of those stores that had a sign, "You break it - You bought it." (I've been in those stores and I always breathe a sigh of relief once I've successfully navigated my way through!)

Well, within a very short time, his son bumped an article and it fell and shattered on the floor. The shop-keeper wanted payment.

What if the father had thought, "I didn't break it. I should just leave and let them deal with my son."

But of course, He would never think that.

Of course, the Father paid for what had been broken.

There are all kinds of broken things in our lives.

Imlay, Nevada

CHAPTER 7   KINTSUGI

There is an ancient Japanese art called "kintsugi" or golden joinery. It is the art of taking a broken vessel and repairing it with gold. This process takes the ordinary and transforms it into a work of art.

It creates a masterpiece out of the pieces of broken pottery.

Imagine that you are in a pottery class and everyone has been given clay to work with. You've all created your own unique bowl on a potter's wheel. Now you are sent home to fire it in your own kiln. Eagerly you anticipate the finished product, but when you pull the bowl from the kiln, it has broken All you have is broken pieces.

But you still have another class to go to, to present your piece for inspection. You place it in a paper bag and enter the classroom with the bravest smile you can muster.

When asked by the instructor how it went, you nod and agree with everyone else that you're very pleased with the result, hoping desperately not to be found out. The conversation around you is enthusiastic but your broken pieces keep calling out to you, and finally you can't handle the charade any longer.

"Mine broke!" you cry out with tears in your eyes. "I don't know what happened. It completely broke! It's ruined!"

The instructor calls you forward so she can examine your work.

She smiles. She knew.

She knew the nature of the clay she had given out. She knew it would break in the fire. Slowly the others in the class also present their broken pieces. Everyone had been caught up in the charade.

She knew. But the purpose of the class was greater than creating perfect bowls. It was to demonstrate the art of kintsugi.

Our brokenness, given into the hands of the "Master Artist", will always be gently held with deep love, and used to create a priceless work of art.

The pain is so real but the restoration is truly priceless.

Germination of the beautiful plant within a seed, can only happen if the seed falls into the ground, dies, and breaks. Then germination can begin and the flower can begin to grow and blossom.

I think we have often looked at "perfect seeds" as some sort of ideal. But God didn't create a finished product. God created seeds. Seeds that needed to break in order to germinate and blossom.

To me this is so encouraging. I've lived far too long thinking that my "breaking" was somehow a second best. But it's not. It is exactly what was intended all along. So that we can blossom.

I'd rather have a flower garden than a bunch of "perfect seeds" any day.

A dear friend of mine restores old cars. He's got several. Every one of these restored beauties are far more valuable than the day they were produced and in their original "perfect" condition.

Another Dear Friend of mine specializes in restoring people.

Ash Springs, Nevada

CHAPTER 8 GRIEF

After we lost the twins, I buried myself in my work. I don't remember talking about it much. We just picked up the pieces and carried on with our lives.

But grief doesn't work that way.

Grief waits.

A year later I really cried for the first time. And even though this happened many years ago, decades in fact, sometimes it still hits me almost like it was yesterday.

I used to think that working through the stages of grief was like peeling an onion and eventually you get to the end of the process. In some ways, it is. In other ways, it's more like doing laundry; there's always another load to deal with.

But I actually find this encouraging. It means we don't have to finish grieving before we can continue living. Our loss will always be with us. Our grief is like walking the rest of our lives with an injury that sometimes flares up. And that's ok; we can continue to live and move forward with our lives while at the same time acknowledging the loss we have experienced. It makes us who we are.

Grieving isn't easy and it takes a long time. It is important to note that everyone grieves in their own way. But we cannot avoid our grief. If we try, it will find a way to confront us.

In our case, my wife and I found ourselves at odds with each other every year around the anniversary of our twins' death, for at least ten years. Once we recognized that pattern, we were able to deal with our conflicts a little better. We began to understand the underlying reason for our conflict.

Often my grief sprang up at the most unexpected times and in unpredictable ways. It would blindside me.

My neatly ordered life began to slowly unravel.

Eventually, through a series of failures and bad decisions, I felt my life completely fall apart. Financial, emotional, spiritual, and relational bankruptcy followed. It felt like God was taking my life apart, brick by brick, and leaving nothing together.

Desperately I sought answers, attempting to keep my life together.

It didn't work. Eventually everything crashed around me. It was on one of those very dark nights that I decided to end it all.

Athabasca Falls, Jasper, Alberta

22

CHAPTER 9   DEPRESSION AND SUICIDE

So little is really understood about how our minds work. And mental illnesses still carry a stigma that makes it hard to accept and admit.

The causes behind depression are as numerous as there are individuals who struggle with it. Sometimes it's temporary and passes after a while; other times it seems to be a lifelong struggle.

But just like any other disease, it can be debilitating and destroy the life of those who struggle with it. It also takes its toll from those who walk alongside us.

Depression has been a constant traveling companion in my life since I was a teenager.

Historically, it appears that depression is often the burden that is carried by some of the most artistic and creative people. Somehow the depths are the inspiration for great things.

I don't presume to speak for others but this is my story.

Since I was a young man, I have experienced many periods of depression, with no light at all. Despair. Utter blackness. If you've been there, you will understand. This is a place where all hope is gone. Only a desperate black spiral going further and further down into the abyss with no possibility of escape.

I understand that from "this side", there is always hope. But when those of us who struggle with this demon are in its clutches, we really do not see any way out.

In those times it really didn't help, to tell me to ask for help. If I thought that there was a possibility of help or if I even mattered, I wouldn't have been in the situation I found myself in.

On better days when I had some hope, I may have believed it was possible. On better days, we may have been able to talk.

But on those dark days, the despair was complete. There was no light in the darkness. I couldn't talk about it.

And I couldn't go on.

I knew I was a failure when even my attempt at suicide didn't succeed. God stopped my hand. Literally! I could not move it any further. My arm was frozen in place.

In His compassion, and against my raging spirit, He spared my life.

I did seek professional help, but anti-depressants made me feel like a zombie. I slept. I had no motivation. I gained weight. Finally, I gave up.

My solution came in the form of a phone call from a friend. He had heard of a vitamin and mineral supplement that helped some people. I tried it and it has saved my life and my marriage. (www.TrueHope.com) This isn't a paid endorsement, nor can I make any promises, but it has helped me.

You may be asking yourself, "What can I do?"

Please, just shine your light of love on us. And if despair claims our lives, do not judge us harshly. We mean to hurt no one. But we simply cannot find the strength to go on.

By the way, I am ok. I just wanted to share my story in hopes of promoting some understanding and to help shed some light in someone's very dark world.

Langdon, Alberta

CHAPTER 10 A FULL MOON

Tonight, in the Nevada desert, I watch as a brilliant full moon rises on a crystal-clear canvas. A chorus of a thousand unseen crickets play their melody through the still night air.

After driving all day, the moon now shines through my window and gently bathes me in its glow.

Throughout my life, I've gazed for hours on this moon. It has taught me much that I identify with. Maybe you do too.

- It has no light of its own. It simply reflects the light of the sun.

- It has a dark side, yet it is still beautiful.

- Even its bright side has its scars.

- Sometimes it fades to oblivion.

- Sometimes it makes waves!

- Yet, with all that baggage, it still provides light to others.

In many ways, we are like the moon. I find comfort in that.

But sometimes I forget.

I'm grateful that it comes around every month to remind me.

Peace, Be Still

Mark 4:39 ASV

Wells, Nevada

CHAPTER 11   WINE

I love wine. I love drinking wine, especially with friends. Of course, too much of a good thing is still too much. I'm talking about the wine, not the friends!

I love making wine. It's the perfect combination of science and art.

I'm no wine connoisseur, but I enjoy a nice glass of wine.

Several years ago, my wife and I had the opportunity to travel to the Hunter Valley in Australia. It is home to one of the best-known wine regions of Australia. Of course, we took a wine tour.

This was no ordinary wine tour thanks to Hunter Valley Horses. www.HunterValleyHorses.com

Spending a day in our own private horse drawn carriage as we visited one amazing vineyard after another created a memory of a lifetime.

At our last winery, I finally asked a question that had been building up in my mind for quite some time.

"Often we hear that the taste of wine is drastically effected by the region that it comes from, and also the year it is produced. What is that all about?"

Our host was very gracious in his answer.

"The differences you are tasting is actually the terra; the earth. The best way for me to explain it, is to show you."

Then he poured several glasses of wine.

First, he took two bottles of Chardonnay. Identical grapes, identical years, the same vintner; everything was identical about these two bottles except for the region they came from. One was from Adelaide Hills, a region in South Australia. The second was from the Hunter Valley, a region just north of Sydney, in New South Wales.

The first wine, from Adelaide Hills, was pleasant, easy to drink, light. In contrast, the Chardonnay from the Hunter Valley, was much more robust and full-bodied. One would either like it a lot, or not at all. It left very little room for an uncommitted response.

Next our host poured a Shiraz from each area. Like before, the wines were identical except for their location. The results were the same. Adelaide Hills had produced a pleasant, easy to drink, light wine. The Hunter Valley, a robust, full-bodied character.

What had caused the difference?

Our host went on to explain that, in that year, the weather in Adelaide Hills had been pleasant. Lots of rain and moderate temperatures had allowed the grape vines to produce abundance with relative ease. It had been an unchallenging year.

The Hunter Valley, however, had experienced harsh weather. Severe drought and scorching heat had forced the vines to struggle mightily to produce their grapes.

The character of the wine had been directly impacted by the respective ease and agony of the year.

How similar is that to the experience of our lives!

Great character is forged on the anvil of adversity.

Langdon, Alberta

CHAPTER 12   DIAMONDS AND RICE

Diamonds are forever, but rice makes forever possible.

I remember seeing a champagne diamond once that was incredibly spectacular even to my untrained eye. Its value was evident to anyone who cared to really look at it. It was arguably the most beautiful diamond I had ever seen.

I don't think of rice that way. Rice is just rice. Yet it sustains the life of billions of people through its nourishment.

Isn't it interesting what we value?

I have had the opportunity to be an executive and I have had the opportunity to be a farm labourer. I have held many positions along that spectrum. Some esteemed. Some very humble.

To be honest, the high-profile positions hold much more attraction for me than the humble service of a position that doesn't get noticed. That is, it doesn't get noticed unless it is not done.

As I've looked around I've seen that most work is humble service that gets very little praise and yet, like rice, it sustains the masses.

I once met a lady whose job it was to clean the private restrooms and showers in a truck stop. It was about 9:00 in the morning and there had already been over 150 showers taken that morning. After each one, she would go in and completely clean and sanitize the rooms.

I thanked her for her service to the truck drivers who passed through.

Her reply was straightforward and enlightening. "I enjoy doing it."

What a wonderful, humble, servant heart!

Her service makes forever possible. It lightens the load of the road for many, and on those days, it's worth more than diamonds.

Rockyview County, Alberta

CHAPTER 13 RED WINE AND JAZZ

The overcast grey sky reflects the state of my spirit over the last while. I haven't written for a long time. I guess I didn't know what to say. Now I just want to talk a bit. Hopefully I make sense.

As evening descends on another day, and "Desperado" plays quietly in the background, I'm spending one more evening, alone. Of course, I'm not nearly the only one.

As I write this, we around the world struggle with a global pandemic, and no one really knows what to do. But we isolate, hoping that will bring us relief.

So, we are alone.

Actually, many of us are always alone. We live isolated lives. Sometimes through choice. Sometimes through circumstance.

But we are alone. We eat alone. We sleep alone. We wake up alone.

And empty.

No, not everyone who lives alone is in need of someone. I'm not saying that.

But our hearts ache.

Or maybe it's just me. But I don't think so.

So, I open the wine and turn on some jazz. I wasn't always a huge jazz fan, but there's something about the soulful notes that soothes my heart.

I prefer red wine. I'm not sure why. Maybe it's just habit.

Tomorrow is Good Friday. It's a day to honor Jesus' willingness to endure a Roman crucifixion to demonstrate the length to which He will go to restore our relationship with God.

On the night before, Jesus ate with his followers. He shared a meal, and bread, and wine. It was a Jewish Passover meal. I wish I understood it better. At the end of the meal he said he wouldn't eat it again until he celebrated it with us in God's kingdom.

If what I've written about the character of God is true, and I believe it is, then God's purpose throughout history has always been to restore our broken relationships: Our relationships with others, our relationship with ourselves, and ultimately our relationship with Him.

And that's what Good Friday and Easter were all about. The hope of an unbroken, restored world.

But it doesn't fix everything here and now.

Here Covid-19 still rages. (It's 2020). Here we lose family, and friends. Here there is still oppression and violence.

Here we still live in a broken world.

But there is hope for a restored future. And there will be wine. And there will be music. And there will be dancing. And "He will wipe every tear from our eyes". Rev 21:4 NIV.

What a gift!

May the Peace of Christ be with you all.

West Coast Trail, British Columbia

Peace Be With You

John 20:21 NIV

CHAPTER 14 ALONE

The evening light
Fades slowly from my room
The trees stand silent
Sentries
Whose shadows move slowly
Across my bedroom floor
The voices of the day
Are silent now
The laughter
A memory
The day is done
And so, the night creeps in
And I am
Alone
Silence
Broken only by my own hands
And the sounds of the night
These are my companions
These and my memories
Memories of love
Of a touch
Of a shared bed

Of your body lying next to mine
Of a time
When the cares of the world
Didn't seem so heavy to bear
But you're not here
And those days are gone
I am alone
My tears are dry
Reduced to a dull ache
I carry in my soul
Sometimes I feel numb
Is there no hope for this restless heart?
Oh, come dear slumber
Embrace me in your arms
Cradle me through the night
And watch over me
Until the light of dawn
Caresses my cheek
And wakes me to face
Another day
And pray perchance
A Love to fill this void

Langdon, Alberta

CHAPTER 15 SUNRISE (DEC 2020)

The sun is rising. I've had my first coffee and the washer just chimed, announcing that the wash cycle is finished.

I'm sitting here thinking of the chaos of this year and the coming Christmas season.

What has caused this chaos? A virus? No, it is fear. Fear of the unknown. Fear for the future. Fear of death.

I am not immune to this fear.

This morning my thoughts were drawn to the verses in Isaiah 41. "Don't be afraid. For I am with you." (Isaiah 41:10 NLT)

This is a promise from the God of the universe.

Whether we believe it or not doesn't change the promise He has made.

There are many times I question His presence.

We all feel alone sometimes.

But His promise still stands. "I am with you… to the end of the age." (Matt 28:20 ESV)

So, in this season of uncertainty, let's look up. Let's simply ask God to make us aware of His presence with us. Let's ask for His help, His comfort, His strength.

The Christmas story is encapsulated in one phrase. "Emmanuel. God is with us." (Matt 1:23 NLT)

That helps me make it through another day.

Rockyview County, Alberta

CHAPTER 16   DO YOU BELIEVE IN CHRISTMAS?

Socrates said, "An unexamined life is not worth living." So, I asked myself a question.

"Do you believe in Christmas?"

Here's the discussion that went on in my head.

"Do you believe in Christmas?"

"Of course I do! I celebrate it every year!"

"Yes, but do you believe in it? It's one thing to celebrate something. It's quite another to believe it."

Seriously, when you really think about it, it's quite a stretch. Mary, a young virgin, gets pregnant. She says she's never been with a man. "It was God who did it." Imagine if she were your daughter. Or imagine you were Joseph, her fiancé. One can hardly blame him for wanting to break off the engagement.

Then angels start to show up. (They had already talked to Mary.) They explain to Joseph that what Mary was saying is true. He agrees to stick with her. When she's due, they find themselves in a stable because all the hotels are full. Together they have their baby.

Then shepherds show up telling of how angels have told them the exciting news. Sometime later astrologers from the East also arrive with expensive gifts, talking of how they were led by some miraculous star.

And then trouble starts. Herod decrees that all baby boys in that area who are under the age of two should be killed. He's heard of this baby who is apparently the king of the Jews. He wants no competition for that title.

And so it goes on. It's a pretty far-fetched tale of escape to Egypt, then return to Nazareth, and then a series of miraculous events: water turned into wine, healing of the sick with a word or a touch, feeding thousands of people with only a boy's lunch, and raising people from the dead.

The story goes on to include his Roman crucifixion where Jesus says, "Father, forgive them. They don't know what they're doing" (Luke 23:34 NLT) and finally Jesus' miraculous rising from the dead.

Do you get the picture? This is an impossible story. It's preposterous!

AND… this Jesus claimed to be GOD!

One would be forgiven for being skeptical.

I asked myself the question again. "Do I believe in it?"

Well, it is a stretch.

Yet we mark our Julian and Gregorian calendars based on these events; BC and AD. (Before Christ and Anno Domini - Latin for "in the year of our Lord")

Clearly it had a significant impact on history and, if the truth be told, it's either all hogwash, or it's true. It's not really more difficult to believe in a virgin birth than it is to believe in resurrection from the dead, or turning water into wine (although with enough wine that might be easier to swallow!)

My point is that once you enter the world of the miraculous, anything is possible.

Anything is possible!

So, what is this story all about anyway? It's the announcement of Emmanuel. God is with us!

Christmas is the beginning of the drama of Jesus' life. A message that God is with us; God is for us; God longs to be in relationship with us; God will never leave us; and God forgives us.

It is only the Judeo-Christian religious tradition that speaks of a Living God who longs to be in relationship with us, and who is continuously striving to reconcile us to Himself.

Now that is a stretch! But what if it's true?

Imagine not ever being really alone - God is with us.

Imagine that no matter how dark the future gets - God is with us.

Imagine the Supreme Being of the Universe whom we call God, knowing each one of us intimately (flaws and all), yet wanting to have a relationship with us.

God is with us!

What if that's true?

Because if it is true, it changes everything, and is the most amazing story ever told.

Imagine the possibility!

Yes, I believe in Christmas, and that is why I celebrate!

Heritage County Park, San Diego, California

CHAPTER 17 SO MANY MILES

By now I've had the opportunity to travel many miles. I've been driving steadily for over three years. When you spend all your time looking out of a windshield you have lots of time to think - and maybe go a little stir-crazy! But it's been a good experience for me.

I'm an extrovert, so it hasn't been easy. I miss being with people.

But it has been good.

Recently I described it as a "beautiful wilderness." It's been a wilderness experience. The isolation, the loneliness, and the fatigue, have been very difficult for me, but they have all served their purpose. I wish this season was over, yet…

Yet what?

Will I miss it? Parts of it, definitely.

There has been a certain freedom that has been precious. I have had so many hours where my mind was free to engage in all kinds of mental discussions - about everything!

And so, I have come to appreciate and value this time for what it is.

And I have grown as a person. No, I'm not bragging. I'm simply acknowledging a fact that I have been witness to. I am not the same person I was when I began this journey.

I have grown to like who I am.

My next chapter tells the story, but for now suffice it to say that this particular part of the journey has been extremely difficult, and worth every bitter tear I cried along the way.

I've made many friends and had some profound conversations with them. They have been sojourners with me - sometimes over a breakfast, sometimes through the wonders of social media.

So where does that leave me now? Do I wish for this desert experience to continue?

No, but I want it to complete in me what it is designed to do. You see, every desert or wilderness has a purpose. These experiences shape us, and if we allow them to, they can produce fruit in us that often cannot be produced in any other way. I wish that weren't true. I wish there was an easier way, but there doesn't seem to be.

So, I embrace it and allow it to change me, and by choosing to embrace it willingly, I protect myself from becoming resentful.

That may sound easy! It may sound as if it's a simple acceptance switch that you put into some positive position.

But it's not. It's a daily choice. And even that sounds too simple. Maybe it's more like a discipline, to not become resentful. To willingly continue on this journey, trying with all my strength to continue to believe that it is working out for my ultimate good - even when it doesn't look like there is hope on the horizon.

I think we often downplay the hopelessness we face. Maybe because we are afraid that if we are honest, it will consume us. Maybe it will.

Unless we open our hands to a Higher Power and trust that our lives are safe in the Hands that have held us before we even knew they existed.

Mucho Lake Provincial Park, British Columbia

CHAPTER 18 THE DAY I BEGAN TO HATE MYSELF

I promised to tell you my story.

It started many years ago. We were taking a family picture. My youngest brother wasn't born yet. I had one younger sister. Everyone else was older.

This is us.

Coaldale, Alberta circa 1959
Photo Credit John J. Unger (my father)

Here is my story.

It's a story of innocence, of condemnation, rejection, and abandonment.

It's a story of isolation, and loneliness.

It's also a story of love, of reunion, and reconciliation.

And a story of victory, and triumph.

I was the victim, and the villain.

I'm sharing it to honor the little boy in the story, and also his journey to become who I am today.

I'm sharing it to celebrate the triumph.

And I'm sharing it with the belief that someone, somewhere, might need to find the little girl or boy that is still waiting for them.

This was the day I started to hate myself.

As we were taking the family picture, I moved.

Taking a family picture was really special. You wanted to get it just right. I was so excited, I couldn't keep my hands still.

And I moved. I ruined it. I ruined the family photo!

That was the beginning.

Recently I read the poem, "Getting There", by Christopher Buckley.

I do not have permission to print it here, but you can read it on-line at: https://www.poetryfoundation.org/poetrymagazine/poems/55545/getting-there-56d23741501ad

After I read it, my story spilled out.

I was driving across the Mojave Desert, somewhere between Bakersfield and Barstow when the truth poured out.

I hated him. I hated my younger self.

No, that's not quite the right word. I despised him. He disgusted me. And I resented him because he would never leave. He always kept hanging around.

Useless. Clumsy.

He cried too easily. He was a wimp. He never kept up. A pest that just wouldn't go away.

And then he would always act up. He'd make comments about things he didn't understand, acting all smart.

And he looked like a joke. Always had puffy eyes either from allergies or because he had been crying. He was so disgusting. And he wouldn't leave.

He still hangs around. This little kid who's always looking for attention. Can't he get enough already?

He's pathetic.

He never got into really big trouble but that's just because he was too cowardly to stand on his own two feet.

Who wants to hang around with somebody like that? No wonder he didn't have any friends.

Yet since he just won't leave maybe I can learn to love him. He is, after all, just a kid.

He's crying. Well, more like deep subdued sobs. Coming from the deepest part of his soul.

"Come here kid. Let's blow your nose."

He blows.

"There. That's better."

He's rubbing the tears from his puffy eyes. His hair is sticking up in the back. Clearly it has a mind of its own.

His jeans are patched and rolled up at the cuff. He's got grubby little hands and is wearing scuffed clodhoppers with laces that have torn and been tied together.

But even through his tears, his eyes shine at the little acceptance I've shown him.

I flip him a couple of bucks and tell him to get us some soft drinks. He comes back with a bunch of packets of Kool-Aid. The kid doesn't know what soft drinks are. I send him back for two soda pops. I pop the tops off, hand him his and take a cool sip of mine. He chokes on the fizz and spills some on his shirt.

"Don't you have any friends?"

He sadly shakes his head.

"Have you ever had any?"

"There was a girl," he tells me. "Back in grade one. We used to play together at recess and at noon hour. But then they told me I couldn't be friends with a girl and needed to play with boys instead.

So finally, I made a friend with a boy. He was in grade six and braided a long rope handle for my lunch kit. It was so long that my lunch kit could touch the floor. But they said he was too old to be my friend. So, I didn't have any more friends for a long time."

We talked for a while after that. He told me how he had ruined a family photo because he was so excited he couldn't sit still. Those were the old days of film, long exposures, and single chances.

He was bouncing his hands up and down when the picture was taken so his hands were a blur.

Eventually he even changed his name.

He's actually an ok kid.

I had to get back to work so I got up and said goodbye. As I turned to go, I caught a glimpse of the hope in his eyes as he asked, "Will you be my friend?"

Tears stung my eyes as I turned away and mumbled, "I'll try."

I wish I had learned to love that little boy sooner. Who knows what we could have become. Yet there may still be time.

Since I wrote this, I've been hanging out with him. He really is amazing. And I love him.

UPDATE:

Since this encounter with my former self, and the acceptance of who he was, I have experienced a profound healing, and it happened at the very instant when I accepted my younger self. I really do like who I have become.

Healing the
Little Boy

Healed the
Older Man

CHAPTER 19 THE CUTTING ROOM FLOOR

Have you ever felt discarded? Kicked to the curb? Thrown out like trash?

I wrote this story many years ago. I'm prompted to include it here in hopes that these truths might resonate with someone who happens to be reading this.

"The King's Daughter"

There was once a kind and generous king who had a very beautiful daughter. Every day she played outside in the sunshine, in the palace gardens. The king loved and adored her.

One day, while nobody was watching, she slipped out of the palace gate, although she had been warned of the danger outside. As she wandered along the streets, she soon lost her way.

Suddenly, two men approached her and recognized her as the king's little princess. They realized the potential for their own gain and persuaded her to come with them. They would help her find her way home. When she agreed to go with them, they bound her and sent a ransom note to the king.

In the meantime, the king in anguish, had realized his daughter was missing and set out immediately to find her. He looked everywhere, but his little princess was gone.

When the ransom note arrived, he immediately tore it open and found the demands were exorbitant. Nevertheless, he quickly gathered what was requested and paid the ransom, as he eagerly anticipated the return of his beautiful daughter.

But the kidnappers were even more wicked than anyone had thought. After receiving their demanded ransom, they continued to hold the king's daughter. They abused her and treated her like a slave.

Days stretched into months and years. Each day, the king in agony, searched for his daughter. He thought of her constantly and longed for her return.

The child grew, and eventually forgot about the palace, her father the king, and her position as a princess. All she knew was her present slavery and the bondage that held her.

Finally, the day came when her captors tired of having her around, stripped her naked and threw her out onto the street as worthless trash.

No one recognized her, but instead anyone who saw her treated her shamefully. They laughed and kicked and scorned her. Who was this wench who wandered about, only in rags?

One day, the king still searching for his princess, saw her and recognized her as his beautiful daughter. Immediately, he went to her and lifted her face to look at him. He saw her pain and his heart was broken again by the abuse she had suffered.

Then through his tears he said, "You are my princess. My daughter! I love you. I have always loved you. I have never stopped looking for you. Now I have finally found you. Will you come home with me?"

Sometimes we feel discarded like that. Used, abused, betrayed, heartbroken, and we begin to believe our "worthlessness." But it's a lie.

We are not forgotten. We are not worthless. Our Father's love for us is without limit - no matter what we have done or been through.

Healing begins when we reach out for that love.

Ripon, California

CHAPTER 20   LIFE'S A DANCE

I love dancing. I told you that earlier in the book. Even as I drive, I often think back to the times when we would dance together.

I wish I was better at it, but I love it. I love the closeness and the movement of two people who are so in sync with each other.

What makes it so magical?

First, the man, who is the lead, escorts his partner onto the dance floor. No, actually it starts before that. It starts with the invitation to dance.

"May I have this dance, please?" This, coupled with the inviting, outstretched hand.

She accepts as she reaches for his hand, and he leads her onto the floor.

Then he creates the frame. Standing tall, he lifts his arms in the classic dance pose.

Here it's important to remember that he leads the dance. This doesn't make him superior. It simply makes him the lead. His job is to lead her in such a way that all eyes will be focused on her. She is the one who receives the attention, and the admiring looks. He orchestrates this performance.

Now he stands inviting her to step into his embrace. She determines how intimate that embrace will be. He honors her.

The music starts and he begins to move. She follows his lead.

This is not the same as a well-practiced and choreographed piece where each dancer moves on their own. That can be beautiful but misses the secret ingredient of the "follow".

To follow she must tune into his subtle signals. A slight nudge on her back. A raised hand. He does not push her. He invites her to move, and she responds.

And if she misses a cue, he recovers in such a way that no one would notice. She is the star.

And they float on air as they travel across the dance floor; sometimes slow; sometimes with charged energy!

And it is magic.

But that's not how a father dances with his young daughter. No, as a very young child, she will stand on daddy's feet, and he will lead her across the floor. His steps will be small and the scuffs on his polished shoes will go unnoticed. He is dancing with his daughter.

Yet as she grows, the dance will change, until the day she dances in the embrace of her lover.

And it is magic.

It seems to me, that this is a picture of how our relationship with God can grow.

It starts out like a father dancing with his young daughter, and we stand on His feet in order to move the way He wants us to.

But then the relationship grows and takes on an entirely new level of intimacy. We become sensitive to the gentle nudging of His Spirit, and we move in Love.

Our lives become one with Love itself. Love is our very breath. Love is our life. And it's magic.

But not always.

Beaver Dam Flats, Calgary, Alberta
Photo Credit: Diane Unger

CHAPTER 21

STILL WAITING

Where is God when we cry to Him and our prayers bounce off the ceiling as if it were a brass reflector, mocking us for our feeble attempts to reach out to God?

And yet we wait. We pray. We cry out. And somewhere deep inside us we believe that God is not silent. We just don't see Him or hear Him.

Because He promised to never leave us or forsake us.

He promised.

He promised.

HE PROMISED!

And we will dance!

"For I know the plans I have for you", declares the Lord, "plans to prosper you and not to harm you, plans to give you a hope and a future."

Jeremiah 29:11 NIV

Buttonwillow, California

EPILOGUE

You are the breath of life
You are the wind beneath my wings
You are the air that I breathe
You are my Eternal Lover
You are my God

The Lord bless you and keep you; the Lord make His face to shine on you and be gracious to you; The Lord turn His face toward you and give you peace.

Numbers 6:24-26 NIV

Malibu, California

AFTERWORD

Tonight, I lie here amazed. So much is happening so fast for me, and for those around me, and I see God's hand so clearly involved in our lives. I've spent the best part of four years driving an eighteen-wheeler across parts of Canada and the United States. If it hadn't been for that period in my life, this book would never have come into existence.

A few months ago, I came to the understanding that my time as a long-haul truck driver was nearing the end. I didn't know what was next, but I let my employer know that I would be leaving.

On the last day of my last trip, I got a call, in response to a resume I had sent out. A week later I found myself in training to drive a 400-ton mining truck.

My journey to this place was not planned - at least not by me. But it has been directed every step of the way by our Heavenly Father. He is the One who has directed the events of my life and even when I have strayed from Him, He has been faithful and has watched over me. He has cared for me.

And He cares for you.

That's a favorite saying of Jonathan Biggs, son of Stan Biggs who took the cover photo and wrote the foreword for this book. Jonathan is a young man with deep insight, and the most sensitive spirit you could ever wish to meet. He has a very special gift. Some would call it Down's Syndrome but his spiritual connection to the Father is remarkable.

What does tomorrow hold?

Life is a journey that takes us along many unexpected pathways. There are twists and turns in the journey that we do not understand. They throw us into chaos. They break our hearts. They cause us to cry out in pain.

But our Heavenly Father knows. He sees. He understands. And He will carry us through.

Because…. "He cares for you."

Printed in the United States
by Baker & Taylor Publisher Services